Come Out to Play, Mr. Blue Jay!

Text by

Robert M. Sanford

Illustrations by

Rebecca Reinhart

Come Out to Play, Mr. Blue Jay!

ISBN 978-1-943424-77-1

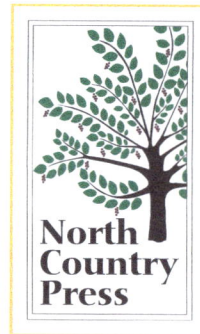

North Country Press
Unity, Maine

Awesome, opossum!

The opossum or possum (Didelphis virginiana) is a marsupial whose population in Maine has increased since the 1990s, likely as a result of warmer winters. Possums eat lots of ticks; they can reach around and catch any that land on them and they will clean out the area they are in, which can mean consumption of a thousand ticks by just one possum in one week. This could help reduce the spread of Lyme disease. They will also eat rats, mice, and cockroaches.

See you later, alligator!

Before 1967, people could bring baby alligators (usually the American alligator, *Alligator mississippiensis*) into Maine without a special license or permit. Of course it was just as bad an idea then as it is now; alligators can grow 12 inches a year whether they are confined in a small aquarium or not. The smaller varieties of crocodilians still grow to at least 5 or 6 feet and are even more aggressive. You can, however, buy an eastern alligator lizard (*Gerrhonotus* spp.), which will stay under a foot long and is not an alligator. Further, it can regrow its tail if need be.

If you wanna, iguana

Pet iguanas require special care or commitment. These non-natives are not capable of surviving our cold seasons outdoors. Pet stores in Maine sell only spiny-tailed iguanas (of the Genus *Ctenosaura*), which are "unrestricted" and allowed as pets.

Really soon, big baboon

The nearest baboon is probably the gelada (*Theropithicus gelada*) at the Bronx Zoo, 435 miles from the heart of Maine. However, this Ethiopian highland species is not a true baboon but looks quite similar. It is kept in the zoo's Baboon Reserve. There is also a Purple Baboon in Belfast, Maine, but that is a gift shop and not a primate. If you were to keep a pair of baboons in Maine, Chapter 7 of the Department of Inland Fisheries' Regulations for Wildlife in Captivity require their cage be 10 feet long by six feet wide by 6 feet high (3 feet longer for every additional baboon).

Neato, mosquito

There are about 40 species of mosquitoes in Maine. About half of the species bite humans. Generally, males feed on flower nectar or plant sap and females bite mammals to get the blood protein for egg production. Mosquitoes can transmit disease to humans and pets. They are attracted by our carbon dioxide exhalations, our body heat, and the smell of our skin. Mosquito control and management is a growing concern, particularly with the risk of potential invasive species like the Asian bush mosquito (*Ades japonicus*) moving into Maine.

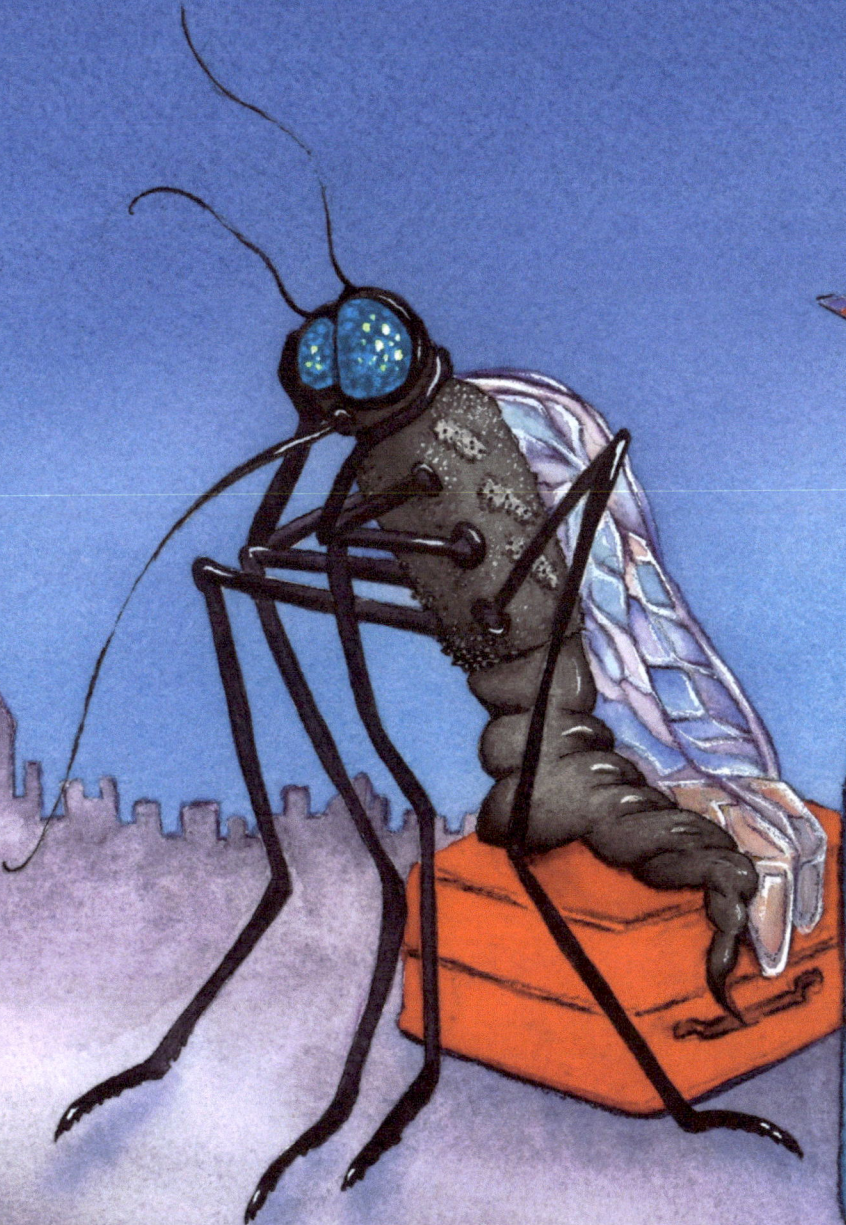

Be right up, little pup

In Maine, a dog should not "be at large" except when used for hunting (7 MRS §3911). When New England was first settled by Europeans one of the first things they did was to set up animal pounds for each town and appoint keepers—this was for all domestic animals, not just dogs. Some of these early pounds have stone walls that can still be seen today. Towns continue to appoint animal control officers. Maine has many Humane Society and other shelters and rescue groups. There are breed-specific places and organizations such as Chesapeake Safe Harbor, Coastal Maine Great Dane Rescue, Second Chance Boxer, and Maine Greyhound Placement Services. Maine Department of Agriculture, Conservation and Forestry provides a list of animal shelters. So does Planet Dog, which also lists dog rescue organizations.

Got a hug, lady bug?

As many as 42 species of ladybugs are found in Maine but only a few species are readily seen. The most common is the multicolored Asian lady beetle (*Harmonia axyridis*), found in a variety of colors from red to yellow. This is the one you may see congregating on the south side of houses in the fall. Ladybugs are helpful to humans because they help control other pests in the garden or household. But some people are allergic to their "dust."

Ladybugs often lay their eggs among aphids, thrips or other small insects so the emerging larvae have a ready food source.

That's a bright tale, white whale

Whale species found off the Coast of Maine include finback whale (*Balaenoptera physalus*), humpback whale (*Megaptera novaeangliae*), North Atlantic right whale (*Eubalaena glacialis*), Minke Whale (*Balaenoptera acutorostrata*), and pilot whale (*Globicephala macrorhynchus* and *Globicephala melas melas*). There are many coastal places for whale watching excursions, but it is important to stay far enough away from the whales to avoid disturbing these magnificent creatures.

You know a victor, boa constrictor

Only 11 species of snakes are in Maine; two of these are subspecies. None are venomous or poisonous. The only endangered snake in Maine is the northern black racer (*Coluber constrictor constrictor*). This snake has a rattle that helps warn predators away and often leads people to believe the snake is a venomous rattlesnake. In 2016, there was a rumor of "Wessie," a large boa or Burmese python that had escaped (or been released) in Westbrook and was reportedly seen at Riverside Park, along the Presumpscot River. Mast Landing Brewing Company even named a beer after it. But the snake was never seen again and could not have survived the winter.

By and by, dragonfly

Maine has 158 dragonfly and damselfly species (they are in the Order *Odenata*). This is a rich diversity. Three of the dragonflies are on the endangered species list. They have some great names: boreal snaketail (*Ophiogomphus colubrinus*), ringed boghaunter (*Williamsonia lintneri*), and rapids clubtail (*Gomphus quadricolor*).

That's the tune, little raccoon

Raccoons (*Procyon lotor*) are common in Maine and do quite well living out in wilderness, but even better in highly populated urban areas, where they thrive off garbage and other easy pickings. Their proximity and adaptability have increased the risk of rabies, a deadly disease that can be transmitted to humans. However, raccoons are interesting and smart animals that continue to appeal to many people.

I'm out the door, dinosaur

No dinosaur fossils have been found in Maine (but chickens are arguably a close relative). Some of the closest dinosaur fossils can be found in surrounding states (but not New Hampshire). *Maine's Fossil Record: The Paleozoic* (2007) by Lisa Churchill-Dickson, published by the Maine Geological Survey, is an excellent resource on what Maine has for fossils.

Yes we oughter, Miss sea otter

The common otter or North American river otter (*Lontra canadensis*) is found in Maine; we probably have about 20,000 of them. Adult females are called "queens" and adult males are "meowters." Family groups are "bevys." These semi-aquatic animals are known for their toughness, intelligence, and playfulness.

Let's hit the road, little toad

The most common and indeed the *only* toad you are likely to find in Maine is the American toad (*Anaxyrus americanus*). Like all toads, it is toxic so most other animals leave it alone. However, it is a garden friend. Its eggs can be seen as curly strands in shallow ponds and take only a week to hatch.

It's not a fuss, hippopotamus

Hippos originated in Africa and were not found in the Americas, although some of their relatives came over during the early Oligocene (34-12 million years ago). However, in 1910, Louisiana Congressman Broussard suggested hippo ranching as a way of handling invasive water hyacinths and providing meat. It didn't work out. Nor do hippos have much to do with Maine, but there is a Hippopotamus Maine steakhouse in Paris (the original Paris, not Paris, Maine). And you can see hippos at the Philadelphia Zoo, about 542 miles from central Maine.

In a few, cockatoo

Cockatoos are parrots in the family *Cacatuidae*. You can get some of them at pet stores. Cockatiels are one example of a cockatoo. Cockatoos tend to get loud and argumentative, and they live a long time. Umbrella cockatoos can live to 60 years and sulphur-crested cockatoos can live to over a hundred. Makes you think before you get one.

Feel free, chickadee

The black-capped chickadee (*Poecile atricapillus*) lives year-round in Maine and is our state bird. We let Massachusetts have it as their state bird too. It has qualities we can admire. It mates for life and stays faithful. The male feeds the mother until the eggs hatch, then they both take care of the young.

Gotta peel, harbor seal

Harbor seals (*Phocidae Phoca*) live along the coast of Maine. The Marine Mammal Protection Act and related efforts have encouraged their rebound from low numbers in the 1970s. Gray seals and harbor seals can be found in our coastal waters year-round—both tolerate the relatively warm waters of the Gulf of Maine. Harp, hooded, and ring seals are more likely to be seen only in the winter months. Very rarely, a bearded seal might show up.

Bye from all of us, walrus

When ice glaciers melted off the coast of Maine some 14,000 years ago, the water was very cold and the habitat was suitable for the Atlantic Walrus. More currently, the Gulf of Maine is too warm for walrus (and is getting ever warmer). The Maine State Museum has some walrus bones and tusks in its holdings.